*GREATER THAN A TOURIST BOOKS ARE ALSO AVAILABLE IN EBOOK AND AUDIOBOOK FORMAT.

Greater Than a Tourist Book Series Reviews from Readers

I think the series is wonderful and beneficial for tourists to get information before visiting the city.

-Seckin Zumbul, Izmir Turkey

I am a world traveler who has read many trip guides but this one really made a difference for me. I would call it a heartfelt creation of a local guide expert instead of just a guide.

-Susy, Isla Holbox, Mexico

New to the area like me, this is a must have!

 -Joe, Bloomington, USA

This is a good series that gets down to it when looking for things to do at your destination without having to read a novel for just a few ideas.

-Rachel, Monterey, USA

Good information to have to plan my trip to this destination.

-Pennie Farrell, Mexico

Great ideas for a port day.

-Mary Martin USA

Aptly titled, you won't just be a tourist after reading this book. You'll be greater than a tourist!

-Alan Warner, Grand Rapids, USA

Even though I only have three days to spend in San Miguel in an upcoming visit, I will use the author's suggestions to guide some of my time there. An easy read - with chapters named to guide me in directions I want to go.

-Robert Catapano, USA

Great insights from a local perspective! Useful information and a very good value!

-Sarah, USA

This series provides an in-depth experience through the eyes of a local. Reading these series will help you to travel the city in with confidence and it'll make your journey a unique one.

-Andrew Teoh, Ipoh, Malaysia

>TOURIST

GREATER THAN A TOURIST- BARBADOS WEST INDIES

50 Travel Tips from a Local

Maria Belgrave

Greater Than a Tourist- Barbados West Indies Copyright © 2021 by CZYK Publishing LLC. All Rights Reserved.

All rights reserved. No part of this book may be reproduced in any form or by any electronic or mechanical means including information storage and retrieval systems, without permission in writing from the author. The only exception is by a reviewer, who may quote short excerpts in a review.

The statements in this book are of the authors and may not be the views of CZYK Publishing or Greater Than a Tourist.
First Edition
Cover designed by: Ivana Stamenkovic
Cover Image: https://pixabay.com/photos/clearwater-villa-beach-barbados-1549544/

CZYK Publishing Since 2011.
CZYKPublishing.com
Greater Than a Tourist

Lock Haven, PA
All rights reserved.
ISBN: 9798412575223

>TOURIST

50 TRAVEL TIPS FROM A LOCAL

>TOURIST

BOOK DESCRIPTION

With travel tips and culture in our guidebooks written by a local, it is never too late to visit Barbados. Greater Than a Tourist - Barbados by Maria Belgrave offers the inside scoop about Barbados. Most travel books tell you how to travel like a tourist. Although there is nothing wrong with that, as part of the 'Greater Than a Tourist' series, this book will give you candid travel tips from someone who has lived at your next travel destination. This guide book will not tell you exact addresses or store hours but instead gives you knowledge that you may not find in other smaller print travel books. Experience cultural, culinary delights, and attractions with the guidance of a Local. Slow down and get to know the people with this invaluable guide. By the time you finish this book, you will be eager and prepared to discover new activities at your next travel destination.

Inside this travel guide book you will find:

Visitor information from a Local
Tour ideas and inspiration
Valuable guidebook information

Greater Than a Tourist- A Travel Guidebook with 50 Travel Tips from a Local. Slow down, stay in one place, and get to know the people and culture. By the time you finish this book, you will be eager and prepared to travel to your next destination.

>TOURIST

OUR STORY

Traveling is a passion of the Greater than a Tourist book series creator. Lisa studied abroad in college, and for their honeymoon Lisa and her husband toured Europe. During her travels to Malta, an older man tried to give her some advice based on his own experience living on the island since he was a young boy. She was not sure if she should talk to the stranger but was interested in his advice. When traveling to some places she was wary to talk to locals because she was afraid that they weren't being genuine. Through her travels, Lisa learned how much locals had to share with tourists. Lisa created the Greater Than a Tourist book series to help connect people with locals. A topic that locals are very passionate about sharing.

>TOURIST

TABLE OF CONTENTS

Book Description
Our Story
Table of Contents
Dedication
About the Author
How to Use This Book
From the Publisher
WELCOME TO > TOURIST
1. Getting around
2. Driving tips
3. How to pay
4. Where to stay
5. Conserve water
6. Enjoy the weather
7. Less is better!
8. Be aware of your surroundings
9. In case of emergency
10. Appreciate our creole
11. A taste of home
12. Experience the fine dining
13. Sample the local cuisine
14. Try the beer and rum
15. Go rum tasting!
16. Sample more rum!

17. Ride the Locomotor
18. Do an island tour
19. Go off-roading
20. Take a hike
21. Submerge yourself
22. Learn about our history
23. Visit the cricket museum
24. Explore a cave
25. Pick a town
26. Catch some Crop Over festivities
27. Oistins Fish Festival
28. Holetown Festival
29. Attend a service
30. Appreciate our wildlife
31. Pack a picnic
32. Experience the nightlife
33. Try horseback riding
34. Go to the races!
35. Visit a cotton field
36. Go souvenir shopping
37. Listen to Steelpan
38. Drink a coconut
39. Enjoy our waters
40. Spot a flying fish
41. Work on your tan
42. Avoid this tree

>TOURIST

43. Lookout for cobblers
44. Protect turtle nests
45. Don't do drugs
46. Camouflage is illegal
47. Places to avoid
48. Appreciate our housing
49. Have an island wedding
50. Your last stop

TOP REASONS TO VISIT BARBADOS

Resources

Packing and Planning Tips

Travel Questions

Travel Bucket List

NOTES

ABOUT THE AUTHOR

Maria Belgrave was born and raised in Barbados where she gained her bachelor's degree from the University of the West Indies in Public Sector Management. She is the mother of one, and she lives centrally in the middle of the island. Maria has a profound appreciation for the outdoors, enjoying activities such as off-roading and exploring. She also enjoys reading, going to the beach, and meeting new people, but occasionally escapes into the world of fantasy through movies and television series.

> TOURIST

HOW TO USE THIS BOOK

The *Greater Than a Tourist* book series was written by someone who has lived in an area for over three months. The goal of this book is to help travelers either dream or experience different locations by providing opinions from a local. The author has made suggestions based on their own experiences. Please check before traveling to the area in case the suggested places are unavailable.

Travel Advisories: As a first step in planning any trip abroad, check the Travel Advisories for your intended destination.
https://travel.state.gov/content/travel/en/traveladvisories/traveladvisories.html

>TOURIST

FROM THE PUBLISHER

Traveling can be one of the most important parts of a person's life. The anticipation and memories that you have are some of the best. As a publisher of the Greater Than a Tourist, as well as the popular *50 Things to Know* book series, we strive to help you learn about new places, spark your imagination, and inspire you. Wherever you are and whatever you do I wish you safe, fun, and inspiring travel.

Lisa Rusczyk Ed. D.
CZYK Publishing

>TOURIST

WELCOME TO
> TOURIST

>TOURIST

"I live where you vacation."

The reaction of most people when they hear about Barbados is "What country is that in?" Barbados, 166 square miles with gentle hills and fields, white beaches and crystal-clear waters, year-round sunshine, and friendly residents is the smallest of a group of islands in the Caribbean. Hotel occupancy is sure to peak between November and February, as tourists trade their winters for the inviting warmth of the tropics. Many will agree that island life is hard to leave behind once you experience the relaxed atmosphere, the culture, cuisine, and the hospitality of the locals (called Barbadians or Bajans). How would you feel waking to the sounds of the ocean every morning, eating fresh fruit with breakfast, lounging by the pool, working on your tan (that will surely be the envy of ALL your friends), taking in the sights, and experiencing everything that Barbados, 'The Gem of the Caribbean' has to offer? Sounds amazing, doesn't it? Well then, let me introduce you to my island!

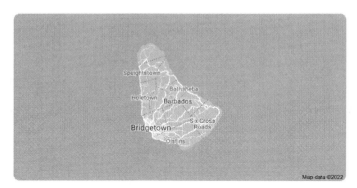

Barbados

Barbados West Indies Climate

	High	Low
January	84	73
February	84	73
March	85	74
April	86	75
May	87	77
June	87	77
July	87	77
August	88	76
September	88	76
October	87	76
November	86	75
December	85	74

GreaterThanaTourist.com

Temperatures are in Fahrenheit degrees.
Source: NOAA

>TOURIST

1. GETTING AROUND

Chances are you will take a taxi to your hotel. Taxis are easily identifiable by their mounted **TAXI** signs, and their license plates begin with the letter **Z**. You should note that taxis are not metered in Barbados; rather, the fee charged is based on distance. Depending on your budget and how often you need to get around, this can be an expensive way to travel. Hiring a private car may be your best bet if only for the convenience, but fuel prices being what they are, this too, could put a small dent in your pocket.

Alternately, there is public transportation in the form of Transport Board Buses (blue with a yellow stripe), Minibuses (yellow with a blue stripe), and Route Taxis or ZRs (white with a maroon stripe). These are assigned to different routes across the island and operate from several stations. Any of these can take you where you want to go, but you will need to know which one(s) to take and you may need to take several buses there and back. Bus fare is charged *per person*, and it is paid **every time** you board a bus, so weigh this mode of transport against your other options, especially if there are other people in your party.

Navigating your way around the public transport system will take some getting used to, but you can seek advice from your hotel's Front Desk. When you board a bus/van, tell either the driver or the conductor (the latter collects the bus fare) what your destination is, and they will be sure to put you at the right stop. Transport Board buses are state-owned and operate on an hourly schedule from 05:00 to 00:00 hours. Minibuses and ZRs are independently owned and run more frequently than buses, but they practice flexible hours.

2. DRIVING TIPS

If you are adventurous and hold a valid driver's license, you may obtain a Barbados driving permit and hire a private car. We drive on the left here, but when in doubt take the lead from the car in front of you. The locals typically stay a safe driving distance away from hired cars as we appreciate that tourists are unfamiliar with our roads and may make some slip-ups. There are just a few things to note when using our roads.

>TOURIST

Under Barbados' laws seatbelts for adults, and car seats for children under five are mandatory. Observe the posted speed limits - 40 km/h in the city, 60 km/h for inhabited areas, and 80 km/h on highways - and adhere to No Parking signs. Use Bluetooth/ handsfree devices with mobile phones or pull over to take/make a call, since it is illegal to use the latter while driving. Under no circumstances should you drive under the influence of alcohol; have a designated driver. Failure to adhere to any of these laws can result in heavy fines.

Always have your driver's license and permit and associated hired documents on your person in case you are engaged in an accident or are pulled over by law enforcement. Never leave valuables in full view in the car; either take them with you, put them in the car's cubby, or store them under the seat. Always lock the vehicle.

City roads and highways are generally in good condition however, the further away you drive from central areas, the smaller and more prone to potholes and disrepair the roads can be. Reduced speed and flashing lights from another driver are an indication that you are given the right of way. Be courteous;

toot your horn as a thank you and proceed with caution.

3. HOW TO PAY

US currency (bills not coins) can be used everywhere in Barbados, and most hotels, restaurants, and businesses accept major credit cards. If you pay by cash, your change will be returned in Barbados dollars and/or coins. Our currency comes in denominations of $2, $5, $10, $20, $50, and $100 bills, and 5c, 10c, 25c, and $1.00 coins. Public transportation uses a cash-only system, and exact fare is recommended for Transport Board Buses as the farebox does not allow for the return of change.

4. WHERE TO STAY

Contrary to what some have been led to believe, Barbados is not a backward, undeveloped country with one room shacks for houses as portrayed in the daytime soap opera "The Bold & the Beautiful" (1996), and more recently in the Netflix series "Outer Banks" (2020). Some of the finest 4-star hotels can be found on the island's South and West coasts, where

>TOURIST

celebrities such as our own home-grown Robyn **'Rihanna'** Fenty (Yes! That's what I said!), Mark Wahlberg, Justin Bieber, Oprah Winfrey, Simon Cowell, David Duchovny, and Christopher **'Ludacris'** Bridges have stayed. If money is not a factor and you want to experience the best Barbados has to offer, compare the rates of our island's more prestigious hotels, and decide what's right for you. There are also budget-friendly hotels that offer practicality and convenience that won't noticeably deplete your savings.

5. CONSERVE WATER

You're probably used to purchasing bottled water for consumption. Here's a fun fact: you can drink Barbados' tap water! Our water is potable and can be used for drinking and cooking. Despite being surrounded by water Barbados is a highly water-scarce island that depends heavily on rainfall to replenish the water supply. During extended periods of drought, districts can be water-deprived for hours, days, and sometimes weeks while water is redirected to other areas. In times of scarcity, our local Barbados Water Authority enforces conservative measures and encourages property owners to invest in water tanks to store and use rainwater to wash cars or water gardens instead of hoses. Your hotel may be one of several green establishments in Barbados and evidence of this will be in your room and surroundings, so while you enjoy your stay in Barbados, reconsider long showers and excessive water use, especially during the summer.

6. ENJOY THE WEATHER

Barbados has two seasons; the dry season which typically runs from January to June, and the wet season that falls between July and December. There is also a *hurricane* season (June-November) during which strong winds, rain, and/or thunderstorms can be expected. Fortunately, the island's unique geographical position spares it from most hurricanes. In 2021, Elsa was the first hurricane to directly impact Barbados since Hurricane Janet wreaked havoc on the island in 1955. We often joke that "God is a Bajan," given the numerous times that Barbados has escaped an impending hurricane with little to no damage.

>TOURIST

In the height of summer, temperatures can reach as high as 89°F during the day. As a tropical island, sandflies and mosquitos may be a bother to people with sensitive skin, so pack your favorite bottle of bug repellent. Cooler temperatures also prevail because I vividly recall a night in January a few years back when I pulled on a pair of socks to warm my toes up. The meteorology office recorded the temperature that night at 64°F. That's cold, for Barbados.

7. LESS IS BETTER!

Shorts! Short sleeves, short pants, halter tops, and sundresses! Regardless of *when* you visit Barbados, you will hardly need so much as a sweater because the nights are warm, and the days are warmer. (You may want to cover up a bit more in the evenings if the bugs and their friends come out to play.) Bring your favorite swimsuits or trunks. There are NO nudist beaches/pools in Barbados, and it is illegal to sunbathe topless or fully naked, as all beaches are publicly accessible. In addition to this, it is also not recommended to enter a store or restaurant in your swimwear; a light wrap/shorts over your bathing suit would suffice. Sunblock is a must if you have fair skin, and especially if you intend to spend lots of time outdoors. Complete your look with flip flops or sneakers, sunglasses, and a hat, grab your camera, and you're ready to explore!

8. BE AWARE OF YOUR SURROUNDINGS

Just as you would at home, let common sense prevail. Do not walk on dark, deserted streets, especially not alone. Be wary of 'friendly' people who approach you without initiation and remember that street characters can be con artists. There is absolutely nothing wrong with making a charitable donation - food or otherwise - to someone who is clearly in a less than the ideal financial situation, but if there is a chance that you will see that person often, be prepared for persistent pestering because they will never forget you.

Avoid night trips to the ATM. Try not to carry lots of cash, and secure your valuables - travel documents and passport, jewelry, extra cash, etc. - in the hotel safe when you go out. While on any outing try not to create an easy opportunity to be mugged,

>TOURIST

especially at the beach. Wallets, cellphones, tablets, watches, even hotel, and car keys are all easy to nab when you are relaxing in the water. Barbados is generally a nice place to visit, but it is not exempt from crime. If the unimaginable happens during your stay, you should know what to do.

9. IN CASE OF EMERGENCY

The locals are typically helpful if you find yourself lost and will advise you on how to get to where you want to be. You should, however, be able to identify the uniformed law enforcement officers of the Barbados Police Force, because you never know when you might need a friendly policeman.

Officers of the Barbados Police Force, in uniform

Most medical emergencies can be handled by the Queen Elizabeth Hospital however, as a state-owned entity, it is almost always overwhelmed, and the wait time can be lengthy. There are several private doctors, medical facilities, and pharmacies scattered across the island should you need such services. Much like the world-renowned '911', Barbados has assigned emergency numbers for its police (211), fire (311), and ambulance (511) departments that can be reached from any mobile phone operating on a local network.

10. APPRECIATE OUR CREOLE

Barbadians speak a quick variation of English that is heavily influenced by Britain. Like many Caribbean islands, Barbados' history reflects a period of slavery during which, forced to abandon their native tongues and learn English, the slaves rebelled by forming their own language much to the dismay of their masters. This language was not abandoned after the abolition of slavery and is spoken by all residents. Known as 'Bajan Dialect,' it can be quite difficult to interpret when heard for the first time.

You may find that to be understood, we mimic your accent when speaking with you, but it is in no

>TOURIST

way intended to mock or insult you. Rather it is merely to make communicating easier, otherwise, we'd have to constantly repeat ourselves. Our dialect can be somewhat ... *colorful* ... if you catch my drift, but again, we mean nothing by it. Now that your bases are covered, let's talk food!

11. A TASTE OF HOME

If you are traveling from the United States and have a hankering for familiar fast food (at one point or another Barbados was home to US franchises KFC, MacDonalds, Subway, Burger King, and Starbucks), you will find a variety of restaurants to satisfy your cravings. From chicken and waffles for breakfast to burgers and fries for lunch, and steak for dinner, there's an establishment that has you covered. Be sure to try the local flagship joint **Chefette** which also offers salads and ice cream in addition to traditional short order options.

Chefette Restaurant, Rockley Christ Church

Some restaurants carry more extensive menus that include appetizers, main courses, desserts, and cocktail choices. There are hundreds of cafes, coffee shops, and mom-and-pop diners littering the island which offer their own unique brand, and you'd be quite surprised at what you may discover.

12. EXPERIENCE THE FINE DINING

Picture it. You and your significant other are on holiday in Barbados. No children, no family, no distractions. Just you and the love of your life on an island paradise. You're thinking, "We should get dressed up and go out to dinner! But where should we go?" Many restaurants offer a succulent mix of Caribbean and seafood dishes, paired with oceanside

>TOURIST

dining, peaceful ambiance, and great food. If you want to take it down *several* notches, but still enjoy a tasty steak, Chefette BBQ Barn is a nice, inexpensive option. The cuisine is diverse in Barbados, so you'll also find restaurants that specialize in Indian, Italian, Mexican, Greek, and Chinese foods, to name a few.

13. SAMPLE THE LOCAL CUISINE

Barbados' national dish is called **Cou Cou and Flying Fish**, made of a unique blend of cornmeal and okras, and the fish is cooked in gravy (or sauce) with onions, garlic, tomatoes, and pepper. The dish is sometimes served with sliced sweet potato, fried plantain, or pickled cucumber, and pairs beautifully with our locally brewed **Banks** beer. Cou Cou can also be made with breadfruit and goes just as well with dolphin, salt fish, or red herring (the latter has a rather strong, acquired taste.) Breadfruit grows seasonally and can also be roasted or fried.

Another island favorite is **pudding and souse**. Seasoned steamed or baked sweet potato is used to make the pudding, and traditionally the souse contains pork and pork pieces (pig ear, snout, feet, etc.) but it can be done with any type of meat. I prefer lean meats in souse, so I opt for either chicken breast, Seacat (the local name for octopus or calamari), or shrimp. Pudding and souse is served with a healthy dose of peppered, pickled cucumber and is usually available on Saturdays.

Other Bajan delicacies include fishcakes and bakes, barbecued pigtails, pickled or fried Seacat, rice and peas, macaroni pie (baked mac and cheese), conkies (seasonal for Independence), sorrel, and jug jug at Christmas time. You'll want to try one or all of these, depending on the time of your visit.

>TOURIST

14. TRY THE BEER AND RUM

Our local beer **Banks** (275ml), "The Beer of Barbados", is also known as the Sheriff, and its sidekick is aptly named **Deputy** (250ml). They boast 4.5% and 4.6% alcohol content respectively and are easily the most popular beers here.

With *four* rum distilleries, Barbados is also home to the world's oldest rum, "the rum that *invented* rum", **Mount Gay Rum**, and other rum varieties such as Cockspur, Malibu, E.S.A. Field, Doorly's, and Old Brigand, to name a few. Our laws allow persons 18+ to drink alcohol but be mindful that it is illegal to drink and drive. Make sure you have a designated driver or arranged transport when you sample our finest. You may be a connoisseur of fine liquors, but never underestimate the potency of our local rum. Alcohol can be purchased from most grocery stores, corner shops, and gas stations.

After you've sampled our rum, become completely fascinated, and you curious to see how it's made, take a tour!

15. GO RUM TASTING!

Mount Gay offers several tours at different locations across the island so choose which one works best for you. I recommend the **Mount Gay Tasting and Lunch Experience** which occurs in the island's northernmost parish of St. Lucy. Bookings are recommended for all tours and for your convenience, hotel collection and return are included. Depending on your tour, you may enjoy a combination of sample tastings and a complimentary cocktail, a trip through the factory, learn how our locally grown sugar cane is used in the production process, and there may even be an opportunity for shopping. Your tour can include 10-12 persons (18+ years) but is not recommended for expecting mothers or persons with serious heart or medical ailments.

>TOURIST

16. SAMPLE MORE RUM!

At the opposite end of the island in St. Philip is the Foursquare Rum Distillery and Heritage Park that produces E.S.A. Field, Doorly's, and Old Brigand rums. This self-guided tour highlights the environmentally friendly functional factory, the rum-making stages, the folk museum, colonial architecture, and historical buildings of Heritage Park. There is no transport accommodation, but there is a play park to engage children while the adults take the tour. Bottles of rum are available for sale and priced cheaper than duty-free storefronts so it might be better to grab a few while you're there.

17. RIDE THE LOCOMOTOR

Take an open-air train ride around the grounds of St. Nicholas Abbey and past the lake on this narrated **Heritage Railway** tour that features stunning countryside views of plantation fields, the East Coast, and the Atlantic Sea. Prepare yourself for the end of the line because I wasn't ready for what happened when a volunteer was requested! (You're curious, aren't you?)

St. Nicholas Abbey is one of the two remaining rum distilleries, with a tour of its own - **St. Nicholas Abbey Heritage Great House and Rum Distillery Tour**. You can opt for this tour instead which showcases the Great House, Syrup Factory, and Rum Distillery (with rum tasting), or combine both tours for the full Abbey experience. Reservations are mandatory.

>TOURIST

18. DO AN ISLAND TOUR

Most taxi operators can accommodate a request for an island tour. No two tours are the same but if you're curious to see the humble house on Rhianna Drive where **Rihanna** was raised, *and* the ocean-front property she purchased at 1 Sandy Lane, you only must ask. Your taxi operator will be familiar with all the best places on the island to sightsee, grab a bite, or shop for knickknacks and souvenirs. On this trip, you might be fortunate enough to see Cove Bay, Hackletons Cliff, Cherry Tree Hill, Bathsheba, Trevor's Way, Farley Hill, Gun Hill Signal Station & Lion, or Culpepper Island, all remarkable sightseeing vantage points. Tours can be personalized to fit your needs and may range from a few hours to a full day's outing so arrange with your guide beforehand to take full advantage of the experience.

19. GO OFF-ROADING

If you've taken the island tour and were awed by the beauty that is Barbados, you'll be super impressed when you experience the country from the backroads. Sign up for one of the safari expeditions if you have an appreciation for nature and like being off the beaten path. These tours use 4X4 trucks to navigate established trails through the wild shrubbery of the island, pausing at strategic points along the way to appreciate the hills and valleys of Barbados. Be prepared for some mud trekking if it rained recently, but the trails are generally uneven dirt roads that make for a rigorous drive. I can throw my weight behind the blended on/off-road **Adventure Safari** which passes through several popular site-seeing locations and ends with lunch. Due to the nature of this tour, it is not recommended for expecting mothers, persons with serious heart or back problems, or other medical ailments, and it is not wheelchair accessible.

>TOURIST

20. TAKE A HIKE

I remember my first hike like it was yesterday; took me nearly two weeks to recover. I started fine, on a downhill trek, then the group turned off the main road, through the shrubbery, meandered a little way, and emerged by a glade of sorts surrounded by banana trees. The tour guide gave us a minute to rest and hydrate, then showed us a solitary house at the top of a very, very steep hill and said that's where we were going next. Now I'm not *totally* out of shape, but I later learned that this trail was used by more experienced hikers.

Luckily, your guided tour need not be so strenuous. Hikes fall into three general categories; the **Stop 'n' Stare** that caters to beginners, the intermediate group **Here 'n' There**, and the **Grin 'n' Bare** for expert hikers. The former may be your best bet, as the tour guide will punctuate it with tidbits of Barbadian history while you enjoy the views, the fresh air, and the company. The bravest of the brave can try the night tour and although this will be quite a different type of experience, the views won't be as impressive.

21. SUBMERGE YOURSELF

Take the standard day or night tour on the **Atlantis Submarine** or opt for the cave exploring excursion on this unique trip down under. My daughter and I took this dive for her 15th birthday and neither of us was prepared for what we saw. We wondered at first how we would board the sub and joked about seeing it docked like a ship is. As it happened, we were taken out into open water on a catamaran and as we watched, the top of the submarine emerged from below. We were somewhat skeptical about crossing from the catamaran to the sub, but once we descended through the hatch into the air-conditioned comfort of the cabin and got settled in, we were ready and raring to go.

While the knowledgeable guide spewed facts about the fish and colonies, the types of coral we saw, *and* a shipwreck the sub sank to an impressive 150 feet. Every seat offered an excellent vantage point and we gazed through the ports on both sides to take in all views. The children on board were especially fascinated with the fish and played a game of "Finding Nemo" among themselves. While this is an excellent tour to experience, I would not recommend

>TOURIST

it for people who fear the dark, or enclosed spaces. I would also reconsider taking children on the night dive as they may not be so comfortable between the period of submersion where the last dredges of sunlight fade and the captain turns on the lights.

22. LEARN ABOUT OUR HISTORY

Barbados was found uninhabited by Captain John Powell in 1625 and he claimed it in the name of King James I of England. He went home with the good news of his discovery and returned to Barbados two years later landing at Holetown, St. James bringing with him ten slaves and eighty settlers. The island has a long history of using enslaved labor to grow tobacco, cotton, and sugarcane, but when slavery was abolished in 1834, the freed citizens educated themselves and sought better jobs while others preferred to remain in the cotton and sugarcane industries.

In 1966 Barbados gained its independence but remained a parliamentary democracy with Queen Elizabeth II as its Head of State. The island celebrated its 55th year of independence in 2021 by releasing its ties to Britain and becoming a republic with its own President and Prime Minister to govern the country's affairs. Through the years its history has been carefully documented and preserved in the **Barbados Museum**, a former British Military Prison located at the Garrison, St. Michael. The museum showcases artifacts of the early inhabitants, furnishings of an 18th-century plantation house, and even a preserved prison cell. Discover the history of the monkey, jucking board, mortar and pestle, rotary phone, and Rediffusion in this self-guided walk-through tour. Touching the artifacts and/or taking pictures is strictly forbidden.

>TOURIST

23. VISIT THE CRICKET MUSEUM

The Cricket Legends of Barbados Museum highlights renowned Barbadian cricketers whose contributions to the sport over the past 100 years came from playing for the West Indies cricket team. If you know your cricketing history, and names like Sir Garfield Sobers, Wes Hall, Gordon Greenidge, Desmond Haynes, and Joel Garner ring any bells, you will want to visit this museum in Bridgetown. As you browse the portrait room and peruse the news clippings and interesting facts about the game, you may be fortunate enough to meet and engage with one of the Legends themselves. Snag a few cricketing paraphernalia from the gift shop and stay for lunch at The Pavilion Bar and Restaurant. The museum is a short ten-minute walk away from the renovated Kensington Oval stadium, where Barbados hosted the World Cup in 2007, and the World Twenty20 finals in 2010. Swing by if you've got a few minutes to spare and take a picture next to the statue of Barbados National Hero, Sir Garfield Sobers.

Kensington Oval, Bridgetown Barbados

24. EXPLORE A CAVE

One of Barbados' biggest tourist attractions is **Harrison's Cave**. A natural limestone formation to a large extent, the cave was renovated in 2018 to allow for easier navigation. The tour is now wheelchair accessible and features interactive displays, improved ventilation, better quality lighting, and a new drainage system. There is also a souvenir shop and provisions for light refreshment.

Visitors travel through the cave in electric trams that take them past descending stalactites and rising stalagmites, columns, alcoves, clear, running streams, deep pools, and a 40-foot waterfall. As you travel

>TOURIST

deeper into the cave marvel as the light reflects off the limestone into thousands of fragments and appreciate the 'natural lighting of the cave' when the guide turns the lights out. Take advantage of every photo opportunity but be sure not to touch anything as the residue on our fingertips - oils, sunscreen, dirt, dust, etc. - can stunt or even kill the growth of the formations. I've taken this tour before and after the renovations and took loads of pictures, but now I wished I had a better camera! I think it's time for another tour.

Harrison's Cave, Allen View, St. Thomas

25. PICK A TOWN

Barbados' main capital, **Bridgetown**, is in the parish of St. Michael with two main streets, **Broad Street**, and **Swan Street**. Bridgetown is the central hub of shopping activity where, as we like to say, "Yuh cud buy from wine to iodine!" Simply put, if you're looking for it, it's sure to be 'in 'town,' if only you know where to look. Broad Street houses an assortment of duty-free shops, malls, department stores, and banks, while smaller family-owned businesses and roadside vendors occupy Swan Street. Bridgetown is easier to navigate on foot.

>TOURIST

There are three other smaller towns - Oistins Christ Church, Holetown St. James, and Speightstown St. Peter. Historically, Oistins served as a trans-shipment site for plantation sugar, but now it features a modern fish market and is considered a fishing community. The location is more of an open-air food court than a shopping center, where several mom-and-pop food shops ply their trade with the catch of the day. Oistins is a hive of activity on Friday and Saturday nights, often with dancing, music, and/or live entertainment.

Holetown is a much smaller, but more upscale version of Bridgetown with Sunset Mall, West Coast Mall, Chattel House Village Shoppes, and Limegrove Lifestyle Centre for your shopping pleasure. You're sure to find something that reflects Barbados' culture and/or history in the chattel village, and you can enjoy duty-free shopping of renowned brands or catch a movie at Limegrove. Unlike the hustle and bustle of Bridgetown, Holetown offers a more relaxed atmosphere, without the crowd.

Speightstown is somewhat of a reflection of Bridgetown with the same type of goods being sold in a similar environment. The town's differentiating quality is several relaxing ocean-front restaurants. After lunch, you can browse the shopping center, sit by the fishing pier, or take a walk along the beach where, although quite nice only attracts the rare sea bather.

>TOURIST

26. CATCH SOME CROP OVER FESTIVITIES

If there is one annual event that attracts tourists from all over the world (even **Rihanna** never misses it) it's Barbados' **Crop Over Festival**, so called because it marks the successful end of the crop season when all the sugar cane has been harvested in preparation for sugar production. The festival generally spans between May and August, and if your vacation occurs at any point during this period, attend some of the events.

The **Opening Gala** and **Ceremonial Delivery of the Last Canes** kick off the celebrations by crowning the King and Queen (the most industrious man and woman) of the festival. There is entertainment in the form of song and dance, eye-catching costumes, decorated carts, and of course, Bajan food on sale.

Bridgetown Market transforms both sides of the Mighty Grynner Highway into one huge open-air market, with stalls selling leather crafts (shoes, bags, coin purses, etc.), local delicacies like fish cakes, and rotis, and even popcorn or cotton candy. You might be lucky enough to see a Tuk-band in action playing its tuk/rukatuk music, or the Barbados Landship in full dance.

The local artists release new soca/calypso music for the season, some that address the issues of the day (called social commentary), and others that lay the foundation of the crop over entertainment for that year. The artists with the best social commentary songs participate in a competition for the **Pic-O-De-Crop Monarch**, and the other songs vie for the honor of becoming **Road March Monarch, Sweet Soca Monarch,** and **Party Monarch**.

Grand Kadooment marks the last of the major celebrations. This carnival parade of sorts is characterized by bands of people dressed in themed costumes, accompanied by music trucks. They dance along a marked route to the Mighty Grynner Highway where there is food, drink, more music, and perhaps a dip in the ocean.

A Crop Over Callender is posted at the beginning of the season citing the locations of activities the whole family can enjoy.

>TOURIST

27. OISTINS FISH FESTIVAL

While Oistins may suffice for a Friday night outing, it does not hold a candle to the full-blown Oistins Fish Festival which occurs during the weekend of Easter. The festival acknowledges all persons involved in the local fishing industry and features several competitions. Watch in awe as competitors vie for the right to boast as the fastest cleaner in the Fish Boning contest or see who can make it to the top of the grease pole (so called because it is slippery).

As you take in the pageantry and art, the music and dance, and the craftsmen selling their wares, be sure to support the festival and try the fish and chips. There will be different types of fish including but not limited to marlin, dolphin, flying fish (seasonal), kingfish, red snapper, billfish, swordfish, and tuna. Fish is normally fried or grilled, sometimes boiled, and served with fries (or other food options), and/or salad.

28. HOLETOWN FESTIVAL

Another great festival to catch if you're in Barbados in mid-February is the Holetown Festival. This week-long occasion begins at the Holetown Monument, by honoring the first settlers of Barbados with a display of local culture and customs. The festival is packed with activities including theatre, street fairs, nightly shows, a Tuk-band parade, antique car showcase, concerts, exhibitions, a fashion show, and lots more. Members of the Barbados Police Force also participate in a tattoo featuring mounted troops, canine, and motorcycle units.

The local artisans take full advantage of the festival to display their leather, woodwork, metal crafts, jewelry, pottery, candles and soaps, and the like. I fell in love with a painting once at Holetown Festival, but it was too big to carry so I arranged to collect it from the gallery the next day. As it was being wrapped, I perused the gallery and found two more pieces *and* a hand-carved bedside lamp that I liked. The festival is a good way for craftsmen to introduce their work to both locals and visitors with the possibility of a sale or two.

>TOURIST

29. ATTEND A SERVICE

Being away from home does not mean that you must forego your worship rituals or practice in secrecy. Barbados is predominately a Christian country, but we respect and embrace all other religions. Denominations of Christianity - Anglican, Methodist, Catholic, Baptist, Moravian, Jehovah's Witness, Protestants, Adventist, Nazarene, Wesleyan, Pentecostal, Church of God, and others - are established here. There are also installments of the Closed Brethren, Rastafarian, Muslim, Jewish, Mormon, Hindu, Baha'i, and the Salvation Army. A quick Google search will show the closest location of your preferred outfit relative to your hotel and it would also be a good opportunity to admire the architecture of these buildings as some of them are over 100 years old.

30. APPRECIATE OUR WILDLIFE

Nestled deep in the mahogany woods of Farley Hill is the closest thing we have to a zoo, the Barbados Wildlife Reserve. You'll find quite a variety of animals here, some indigenous to Barbados, others imported, but all cohabiting the same space.

I visited the reserve in the summer. As soon as I entered, I was greeted with this loud *cracking* type sound which I could not immediately place. As I made my way down the cobblestone path, I realized that the sound was both behind me *and* in front of me at the same time. A little while later I asked an employee about it, and he informed me that it was the height of tortoise mating season (they were all coupling) and the sound I was hearing was the tortoise shells rubbing against each other. Quite the educational moment.

Timid deer lurked behind bushes, two love birds exchanged vows, and alligators floated lazily in the pond and watched me with wary eyes. I was comforted by the fact that the snakes were caged but somewhat disappointed that the peacock didn't display his train because from what I could tell his feathers were gorgeous. Just after 2 p.m., a troop of green monkeys swung into the reserve with loud hoots and screeches, and I soon learned that it was feeding time. This is the best time to be in the reserve otherwise you might miss some of the animals.

31. PACK A PICNIC

When you leave the Wildlife Reserve, you can pop over to the other side of the road to the Farley Hill National Park as you're in the area and kill two birds with one stone. Farley Hill Mansion, built for entertaining royalty in 1879 by Sir Graham Briggs, was used in the filming of the 1957 movie *Island in the Sun* on the fictitious island of Santa Marta. Sadly, the mansion that was once revered as the most impressive in Barbados was gutted in 1965 but the ruins are still surrounded by a forest of mahogany trees and remain a popular spot for picnicking, picture taking, and sightseeing with lovely views of the island's east coast. The spacious grounds are used to host annual concerts such as Reggae on the Hill (April), Gospel Fest (May), and Soca on the Hill (July). The park remains pretty much vacant for the rest of the year except for the occasional picnickers on public holidays.

32. EXPERIENCE THE NIGHTLIFE

I've often heard there's nothing to do at night during the week, but that is not necessarily true. If there's one place on the south coast where there's always activity, it's St. Lawrence Gap. Whether you want to shop, eat, enjoy karaoke, or visit a nightclub, this is the place to be. Bay Street, Bridgetown, and 1st Street, Holetown also offer decent nightlife with clubs playing a mix of music from local and regional calypso/soca to the latest reggae and dancehall, and everything in between. If clubbing is not your scene, and you're looking for a romantic alternative, consider a late evening cruise, a stroll along the Boardwalk, or a movie at Limegrove Cinemas.

>TOURIST

33. TRY HORSEBACK RIDING

Six stables are currently registered to facilitate horseback tours that vary from land and beach riding to swimming with the horses and picnicking after. Groups are small and typically cater to about six persons, led by experienced, knowledgeable guides. Previous riding experience is not necessary because riders are paired with horses with the temperament that matches their riding level.

Bath Beach and Conset Bay in the parish of St. John, and the Scotland District in St. Andrew are all praised as prime locations for horseback riding. Depending on the tour you may see ponds with wild ducks and/or coots, fruit orchards that will hopefully be in season, mongooses, and roaming green monkeys amongst other local flora and fauna. I am deathly afraid of animals that are bigger than I am, but someday I am going to conquer my fear and mount one of these beautiful beasts because horseback riding is on my bucket list.

34. GO TO THE RACES!

A stone's throw away from the Barbados Museum is the Garrison Savannah, a large expanse of turf which serves as a horseracing track, a former cricket ground. The savannah is surrounded by several buildings rooted in deep history including the Clock Tower, the Main Guard House, and George Washington House, so named after the first US President who it is alleged resided there.

Horseracing is a popular, seasonal sport with competitions that draw spectators between January and April, May and September, and November and December. The most notable of them, the Sandy Lane Gold Cup is a renowned racing event that attracts international jockeys, trainers, and thoroughbred owners whose finest horses compete for the honor of winning the prestigious cup. The environment is charged immediately before, during, and after this, the biggest race of the year which remains the topic of discussions for horse racing enthusiasts for weeks after.

>TOURIST

35. VISIT A COTTON FIELD

Did you know that we grow cotton here? Barbados is the home of the popular West Indian Sea Island Cotton (WISIC), the raw product of a combination of the island's unique climate, soil, and geographical location. Unfortunately, it is now grown on a much smaller scale as efforts to revive the cotton industry in Barbados to the heights it once enjoyed were unsuccessful.

Cotton is planted in August and matures between December and January which makes for harvesting in mid-February. The cotton collection is carefully done by hand and the seeds are removed in preparation for export to Switzerland to be spun into yarn, and Italy for weaving into fabrics.

Cotton fields when mature are easy to spot for their white buds bobbing in the wind. Spare a moment to pluck a bud or two, unwrap it from around its seed, and marvel at the softest, silkiest, strongest, high-grade cotton that is used to make luxurious clothing, towels, and sheets.

36. GO SOUVENIR SHOPPING

What makes the best souvenirs? When you go on holiday, what do you take home to remind you of "that time you went to …?" You'll find no shortage of memorabilia to show off your trip to Barbados, T-Shirts and bags, keyrings and bottle openers, aprons and oven mittens, the more common collectibles. But let's broaden your horizon a bit. How about a desk clock or napkin holder in the *shape* of Barbados, abstract carvings made of sanded coconut shells, unique personalized clay pottery, brightly dressed handmade dolls, conch shells, handcrafted metal jewelry, paintings, even confectionery? Intrigued? Located in Bridgetown is a collection of brightly painted souvenir shops known as **Pelican Village** where you can find all the above and more.

>TOURIST

37. LISTEN TO STEELPAN

Although Barbados cannot take credit for the invention of steelpan music (that honor goes to Trinidad & Tobago), we embraced it and made it our own. Steelpans are craftily made from 55-gallon industrial drums, with strategically placed indentations that create different musical notes when struck. An experienced pannist can offer an excellent rendition of any song in any genre, often while playing multiple drums simultaneously. Steelpan music, an indication of a thoroughly Caribbean experience, creates a nice romantic atmosphere when played softly during dinner, a setting many restaurants offer around the island. Steelpan performances are typical during the Crop Over festival, notably **Pan in the City** that is held in Bridgetown, and **Pan Pun de Sand**, a huge beach event.

38. DRINK A COCONUT

When you're out and about discovering and enjoying the island, feel free to stop by a roadside coconut vendor, especially if it's a hot day. Coconuts are green, oblong-shaped fruit with a hard outer shell. The vendor will whittle some of the shell off and punch the soft underlayer so you can drink the water. If you're lucky there may be some jelly inside. Jelly forms from coconut water that remains inside the fruit while it grows over a period and if left long enough, and the fruit is dried, it becomes hard, edible coconut. Jelly can be soft and translucent or firm and chewy depending on the maturity of the coconut. Coconut vendors can also be found close to the beach.

>TOURIST

39. ENJOY OUR WATERS

As a major tourist destination, Barbados offers a wide variety of watersport activities for your enjoyment. Rent a jet ski or waterskis, fly-, foil-, boogie-, paddle- or surfboard, kite or windsurfing equipment, or a kayak and head out for a bit of exhilarating water fun. Snag some snorkeling equipment to better see schools of fish and turtles, or use scuba gear to explore sunken ships, coral reefs, barrel sponges, sea fans, manta and stingrays, and barracuda. You can also view fish and reefs through a glass-bottom boat if you'd rather not get wet or take the family on a catamaran cruise. Whether you're topside or bottom, the experience will be phenomenal.

Snorkeling on a reef

40. SPOT A FLYING FISH

The flying fish, the star of our national dish, and a featured image on the Barbados $1 coin is so called because it propels itself out of the water, giving the appearance that it is flying. With enough momentum, flying fish can glide for up to a whopping 650 feet and use this ability to escape predators.

In recent times the quantity of flying fish that would normally be found in Barbados' waters has drastically declined making the commodity scarce and somewhat more expensive to buy. Theorists blame the decrease on climate change, suggesting that the fish migrated to cooler waters, so count yourself lucky if you are fortunate enough to see a school of flying fish 'take flight' while bathing or enjoying some water sporting activities.

>TOURIST

41. WORK ON YOUR TAN

Sunbathing is a popular pastime for tourists, and while you can work up an enviable tan poolside, why not kill two birds and experience the cool breeze blowing off azure waters, under a parasol, while reading or sipping an island cocktail? The best beaches can arguably be found on the south coast, but since my roots are buried in Christ Church, I may be a bit skewed.

Pebble Beach, Bayshore Beach, and Brownes Beach are all on the same stretch collectively called Carlisle Bay, but with different access points. One long expanse of nothing but pristine white beaches dotted with trees, picnic tables, and sea bathers. You'll hardly see a wave here, even during high tide, and the warm waters are shallow for prime relaxation. Located along Bay Street on the outskirts of Bridgetown, Carlisle Bay is a favorite of the locals, who flock there on Sundays after lunch and especially on public holidays. Similar beaches include **Brandons** and **Dover**.

A short distance away, and the ultimate location for jet skiing and surfing is another favored beach, **Accra** (also known as **Rockley**). Directly across from one branch of Chefette, Accra beach is within walking distance of a small duty-free shopping center, just remember to cover up if you decide to visit a storefront. There is also a boardwalk that is good for jogging, dog walking, taking pictures or just personal reflection as you watch a spectacular island sunset. Silver Sands and Miami beaches are also very popular for watersports.

42. AVOID THIS TREE

As you choose your shady spot beneath the trees and prepare to relax at your beach of choice, be sure to avoid the **manchineel** tree. (I've pronounced this manche-*needle* my whole life, going by how the older folk spoke.) These trees reach heights of up to 45 feet, with dark gray bark and white-green flowers. The fruit resembles a small green apple, greenish-yellow when ripe. Every part of this tree, including the bark and its shiny green leaves, is poisonous. Do not be fooled by the fragrance it emanates, and do not seek shelter under it during rainfall. Ingestion causes the throat and stomach to blister, swell, and bleed and ultimately leads to death.

>TOURIST

The leaves and fruit of the manchineel tree

43. LOOKOUT FOR COBBLERS

While some people like to lounge and swim at the beach, others like to explore. Sometimes hidden among shallow, rocky shorelines, and occasionally lurking on reefs, you may find a black sea urchin, what we call a **cobbler**. At some beaches during low tide, flat rocks are exposed when the tide goes out. The pools of water that remain between the rocks sometimes trap little fish that must wait until the tide comes in again. Children specially, are often fascinated by this and may want to go exploring.

Cobblers are small black balls covered with long spikes that can be somewhat camouflaged among the rocks. The spikes will likely remain in the foot if

75

stepped on, and you will need to seek medical attention. Cobblers are similar in appearance to the *white* sea egg which is a seasonal delicacy in Barbados.

Spikey cobbler

44. PROTECT TURTLE NESTS

Barbados is the nesting place of both the Hawksbill and Leatherback turtles. Between April and November, the Hawksbill lays its eggs mainly on the south and west coasts of the island, while the Leatherback prefers to nest on the east and south coasts between February and July. These species are endangered as they have always been hunted for their eggs, shells, and meat, and their numbers are now much depleted.

>TOURIST

Turtles are fiercely protected by law in Barbados to the extent that persons may be fined up to $50,000 or sentenced to serve a 2-year prison term, *or both*, if they are found guilty of buying/selling or catching a turtle(s), or disturbing/endangering or removing the eggs.

45. DON'T DO DRUGS

Barbados' legislation is extremely clear on drug use. Prescription and/or legally sold over-the-counter drugs will not draw any attention from the authorities, however, the use of drugs for *recreational* purposes (marijuana, cocaine, heroin, etc.) is illegal and punishable by law. Cigarettes and vaping devices are allowed, but only in areas where other people are unlikely to be affected. Some restaurants have smoking and non-smoking sections for everyone's convenience.

46. CAMOUFLAGE IS ILLEGAL

Several years ago, when I was much younger and didn't know better, I was walking through Bridgetown in a camouflage shirt I had recently bought in St. Lucia when I was flanked by two officers of the Barbados Defence Force wearing full camouflage garb. The one on my left asked if I knew it was illegal to wear camouflage. Before I could answer, the one on my right said they would be within their right to "remove me from the street and confiscate my shirt." Ignorance certainly was not bliss just then, so when I got safely home, I did my research.

Camouflage, in either black, blue, green, or gray, is illegal in *any* form or fashion, clothing or otherwise, and may result in a fine or seizure of said items. In Barbados, camouflage is to be worn only by members of our Barbados Defence Force. Failure to comply can result in a fine of $2000 or a year's imprisonment.

>TOURIST

47. PLACES TO AVOID

As with any country, there are undesirable areas that are best left unseen. In the densely populated areas of Bridgetown, where street smarts far outweigh formal academic training, where certain activities are a way of life just to ensure survival, and where opportunists are plenty, active, and lurking, it would be wise to avoid these areas altogether. They are easily identifiable, especially at night.

They will most likely be crowded and characterized by loud, questionable music (mostly dancehall that promotes violence), lots of bars, ladies of the night, games of chance, and extreme profanity. If you absolutely MUST pass through one of these areas while walking, do not walk alone, avoid the darker streets, and do not be conned by heart-wrenching stories that appeal to your better nature. Speak if spoken to but keep moving, and never let on that you are a tourist and/or afraid. If you are driving through, keep the windows up and the doors locked.

Some people may identify with and feel right at home in this atmosphere, more so than anywhere else, and that is okay. To each his own but be mindful that in these neighborhoods, opportunities are seldom missed, and you may be a chance for a payday.

48. APPRECIATE OUR HOUSING

The first dwellings in Barbados were called chattel houses and they were inhabited by plantation workers. They were wooden structures with gable roofs and jalousie windows settled atop blocks and were so called because they could easily be moved. Despite advances in architecture, chattel houses still dot the housing landscape, mostly in sad states of disrepair, but others immaculately restored and maintained, standing proudly as reminders of our history.

Well maintained chattel house

Over the years the type and size of housing structures evolved and now there is an assortment of modest brick houses and housing units, apartment blocks and high-rise complexes, gated communities, and affluent mansions complete with pools and other modern luxuries.

49. HAVE AN ISLAND WEDDING

Barbados is the kind of island that you fall in love with again, and again, and again. Imagine one of the most important days of your life, your wedding day, spun as the ultimate idyllic fairy tale in Barbados. Beach wedding? Sure. Lush garden wedding? Of course! You can even be married in our own Harrisons Cave. Indoors, outdoors, poolside, cliff view, ocean view, traditional or island-inspired, whatever you want, *however* you want it, the perfect wedding can happen, here.

Several hotels offer wedding packages, but other locations across the island cater specifically to the exchange of nuptials. Team up with a wedding planner and start the ball rolling. Getting hitched in Barbados is almost hassle-free. To apply for a marriage license you will need your birth certificate and passport, a letter of intent to perform the ceremony from a Magistrate, and if previously married, the original marriage, divorce, or death certificates. Since Barbados is also a top-rated honeymoon destination, you may want to skip the ceremony and come for the romance.

50. YOUR LAST STOP

You're checked in at the airport with a few hours to kill before takeoff and your visit to Barbados is now almost over. Grantley Adams International Airport, the only airport on the island has restaurants and duty-free shops to keep you engaged until it's time to head out. If you didn't get a chance to, now's the time to snag a few trinkets to remember your holiday, or souvenirs for your loved ones back home. Be sure to keep track of the time though, or you'll hear your name being called for boarding over the PA system!

I can say with surety that you will enjoy your time here so start planning your trip to Barbados. See you soon!

>TOURIST

TOP REASONS TO VISIT BARBADOS

- Inescapable island life that is ingrained in every aspect of day-to-day activities.

- The hospitality of the people.

- Engaging activities for all members of the family.

>TOURIST
RESOURCES

http://www.barbadosseaturtles.org/pages/resources/outreach.html
https://14755.partner.viator.com/tours/Barbados/Mount-Gay-Signature-Rum-Tour-with-Lunch/d30-39983P3
https://barbados.org/barbados-beaches-nude-bathing.htm#.YcyDDGjMLIU
https://barbados.org/barbados-watersports.htm#.Yeqlrf7MLIU
https://barbados.org/blog/steel-pan-music-in-barbados/#.YesH0_7MLIU
https://barbados.org/chattel.htm#.Yd4Elv7MLIU
https://barbados.org/coconuts/coconut-vendor.htm#.YesJmP7MLIU
https://barbados.org/cotton.htm#.YdSkNWjMLIU
https://barbados.org/cropover.htm#.YdOkjWjMLIU
https://barbados.org/currency.htm#.YcuLLmjMLIU
https://barbados.org/fhill.htm#.Yer2tf7MLIU
https://barbados.org/foursquare-rum-distillery.htm#.YdCZFWjMLIU
https://barbados.org/hcave.htm#.YeroWf7MLIU
https://barbados.org/holetown.htm#.YeAtUv7MLIX
https://barbados.org/htown.htm#.YdMBomjMLIU
https://barbados.org/legends-barbados-cricket-museum.htm#.Yerm7P7MLIU
https://barbados.org/museum2.htm
https://barbados.org/music/steel-pan.htm#.YesH0P7MLIU
https://barbados.org/off.htm#.Yd7mY_7MLIV
https://barbados.org/oistins.htm#.Yc8ZwWjMLIU
https://barbados.org/pelican_village.htm#.YesHVP7MLIU
https://barbados.org/reserve.htm#.Yer2j_7MLIU
https://barbados.org/scenic.htm#.YdJv_mjMLIU
https://barbados.org/spght.htm#.YdMFOWjMLIU
https://barbados.org/weather.htm#.YcunXGjMLIU
https://barbados.org/weddings.htm#.YeHS5P7MLIU

https://barbadostoday.bb/2020/01/06/rihanna-mark-wahlberg-and-18-other-celebs-who-love-to-vacation-in-barbados/
https://barbadostoday.bb/2020/04/27/rbpf-restriction-on-wearing-of-camouflage/
https://barbadoswaterauthority.com/
https://en.wikivoyage.org/wiki/Diving_in_Barbados/Cobblers_Reef#:~:text=In%20Barbados%20long%20spined%2C%20black,take%20the%20edible%20Sea%20Eggs
https://premierattractions.bb/barbados-a-little-insider-information-10-things-to-know/#.YdCTf2jMLIX
https://travel.gc.ca/destinations/barbados?wbdisable=true
https://www.barbados.atlantissubmarines.com/submarine-day-dive
https://www.barbadospocketguide.com/art-and-culture-in-barbados/festivals/oistins-fish-festival.html
https://www.barbadospocketguide.com/getting-around-in-barbados.html
https://www.barbadospocketguide.com/our-island-barbados/about-barbados/bajan-dialect.html#:~:text=Bajan%20dialect%20is%20a%20unique,and%20forced%20to%20speak%20English
https://www.barbadospocketguide.com/our-island-barbados/emergency-services.html
https://www.barbadospocketguide.com/our-island-barbados/history-of-barbados.html
https://www.barbadospocketguide.com/our-island-barbados/plants/crops/sea-island-cotton.html
https://www.barbadospocketguide.com/sports-in-barbados/sporting-events/hike-barbados.html
https://www.best-barbados-beaches.com/manchineel-trees.html
https://www.gov.bb/marriage-licence
https://www.hotels.com/go/barbados/best-nightlife-barbados
https://www.nwf.org/Educational-Resources/Wildlife-Guide/Fish/Flying-Fish
https://www.orbzii.com/guides-tips/horse-riding-barbados/

>TOURIST

https://www.planetware.com/barbados/top-rated-beaches-in-barbados-bar-1-4.htm
https://www.sandals.com/blog/barbados-foods-drinks/
https://www.sixt.co.uk/magazine/tips/driving-tips-barbados/#:~:text=There%20is%20no%20Blood%20Alcohol,of%20a%20hands%2Dfree%20system.
https://www.sunsetcrestbarbados.com/shopping
https://www.thebrokebackpacker.com/is-barbados-safe/
https://www.timeoutbarbados.com/blog/104-10-essentials-to-pack-when-visiting-barbados.html
https://www.tobaccocontrollaws.org/legislation/country/barbados/summary#:~:text=Smoking%20is%20prohibited%20in%20all,%2C%20workplaces%2C%20and%20cultural%20sites
https://www.totallybarbados.com/articles/about-barbados/religion-in-barbados/
https://www.viator.com/tours/Barbados/Adventure-Safari/d30-322796P10
https://www.viator.com/tours/Barbados/St-Nicholas-Abbey-Heritage-Railway/d30-149667P1
https://www.viator.com/tours/Barbados/St-Nicholas-Abbey-Heritage-Great-House-and-Rum-Distillery-Tour/d30-149667P2
https://www.visitbarbados.org/bridgetown
https://www.visitbarbados.org/farley-hill-national-park
https://www.visitbarbados.org/the-garrison-savannah

The island of Barbados
https://www.mapsofworld.com/barbados/

Videos
Limegrove Lifestyle Centre
https://youtu.be/t_76kCv46JM

Manchineel: The most deadly tree in the world
https://www.youtube.com/watch?v=uct8H9kV47g

50 Locations Above Barbados
https://www.youtube.com/watch?v=XjEfVxTuXUw

>TOURIST

PACKING AND PLANNING TIPS

A Week before Leaving

- Arrange for someone to take care of pets and water plants.
- Email and Print important Documents.
- Get Visa and vaccines if needed.
- Check for travel warnings.
- Stop mail and newspaper.
- Notify Credit Card companies where you are going.
- Passports and photo identification is up to date.
- Pay bills.
- Copy important items and download travel Apps.
- Start collecting small bills for tips.
- Have post office hold mail while you are away.
- Check weather for the week.
- Car inspected, oil is changed, and tires have the correct pressure.
- Check airline luggage restrictions.
- Download Apps needed for your trip.

Right Before Leaving

- Contact bank and credit cards to tell them your location.
- Clean out refrigerator.
- Empty garbage cans.
- Lock windows.
- Make sure you have the proper identification with you.
- Bring cash for tips.
- Remember travel documents.
- Lock door behind you.
- Remember wallet.
- Unplug items in house and pack chargers.
- Change your thermostat settings.
- Charge electronics, and prepare camera memory cards.

>TOURIST

READ OTHER GREATER THAN A TOURIST BOOKS

Greater Than a Tourist- California: 50 Travel Tips from Locals

Greater Than a Tourist- Salem Massachusetts USA 50 Travel Tips from a Local by Danielle Lasher

Greater Than a Tourist United States: 50 Travel Tips from Locals

Greater Than a Tourist- St. Croix US Birgin Islands USA: 50 Travel Tips from a Local by Tracy Birdsall

Greater Than a Tourist- Montana: 50 Travel Tips from a Local by Laurie White

Children's Book: Charlie the Cavalier Travels the World by Lisa Rusczyk Ed. D.

> TOURIST

Follow us on Instagram for beautiful travel images:
http://Instagram.com/GreaterThanATourist

Follow *Greater Than a Tourist* on Amazon.

CZYKPublishing.com

At *Greater Than a Tourist*, we love to share travel tips with you. How did we do? What guidance do you have for how we can give you better advice for your next trip? Please send your feedback to GreaterThanaTourist@gmail.com as we continue to improve the series. We appreciate your constructive feedback. Thank you.

>TOURIST

METRIC CONVERSIONS

TEMPERATURE

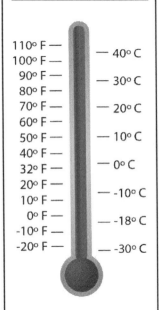

110° F — — 40° C
100° F —
90° F — — 30° C
80° F —
70° F — — 20° C
60° F —
50° F — — 10° C
40° F —
32° F — — 0° C
20° F —
10° F — — -10° C
0° F — — -18° C
-10° F —
-20° F — — -30° C

To convert F to C:

Subtract 32, and then multiply by 5/9 or .5555.

To Convert C to F:

Multiply by 1.8
and then add 32.

32F = 0C

LIQUID VOLUME

To Convert:................Multiply by
U.S. Gallons to Liters................. 3.8
U.S. Liters to Gallons 26
Imperial Gallons to U.S. Gallons 1.2
Imperial Gallons to Liters....... 4.55
Liters to Imperial Gallons 22
1 Liter = .26 U.S. Gallon
1 U.S. Gallon = 3.8 Liters

DISTANCE

To convert ....Multiply by
Inches to Centimeters 2.54
Centimeters to Inches 39
Feet to Meters...................... .3
Meters to Feet 3.28
Yards to Meters 91
Meters to Yards 1.09
Miles to Kilometers 1.61
Kilometers to Miles............ .62
1 Mile = 1.6 km
1 km = .62 Miles

WEIGHT

1 Ounce = .28 Grams
1 Pound = .4555 Kilograms
1 Gram = .04 Ounce
1 Kilogram = 2.2 Pounds

>TOURIST

TRAVEL QUESTIONS

- Do you bring presents home to family or friends after a vacation?
- Do you get motion sick?
- Do you have a favorite billboard?
- Do you know what to do if there is a flat tire?
- Do you like a sun roof open?
- Do you like to eat in the car?
- Do you like to wear sun glasses in the car?
- Do you like toppings on your ice cream?
- Do you use public bathrooms?
- Did you bring a cell phone and does it have power?
- Do you have a form of identification with you?
- Have you ever been pulled over by a cop?
- Have you ever given money to a stranger on a road trip?
- Have you ever taken a road trip with animals?
- Have you ever gone on a vacation alone?
- Have you ever run out of gas?

- If you could move to any place in the world, where would it be?
- If you could travel anywhere in the world, where would you travel?
- If you could travel in any vehicle, which one would it be?
- If you had three things to wish for from a magic genie, what would they be?
- If you have a driver's license, how many times did it take you to pass the test?
- What are you the most afraid of on vacation?
- What do you want to get away from the most when you are on vacation?
- What foods smell bad to you?
- What item do you bring on ever trip with you away from home?
- What makes you sleepy?
- What song would you love to hear on the radio when you're cruising on the highway?
- What travel job would you want the least?
- What will you miss most while you are away from home?
- What is something you always wanted to try?

>TOURIST

- What is the best road side attraction that you ever saw?
- What is the farthest distance you ever biked?
- What is the farthest distance you ever walked?
- What is the weirdest thing you needed to buy while on vacation?
- What is your favorite candy?
- What is your favorite color car?
- What is your favorite family vacation?
- What is your favorite food?
- What is your favorite gas station drink or food?
- What is your favorite license plate design?
- What is your favorite restaurant?
- What is your favorite smell?
- What is your favorite song?
- What is your favorite sound that nature makes?
- What is your favorite thing to bring home from a vacation?
- What is your favorite vacation with friends?
- What is your favorite way to relax?
- Where is the farthest place you ever traveled in a car?

- Where is the farthest place you ever went North, South, East and West?
- Where is your favorite place in the world?
- Who is your favorite singer?
- Who taught you how to drive?
- Who will you miss the most while you are away?
- Who if the first person you will contact when you get to your destination?
- Who brought you on your first vacation?
- Who likes to travel the most in your life?
- Would you rather be hot or cold?
- Would you rather drive above, below, or at the speed limited?
- Would you rather drive on a highway or a back road?
- Would you rather go on a train or a boat?
- Would you rather go to the beach or the woods?

>TOURIST

TRAVEL BUCKET LIST

1.

2.

3.

4.

5.

6.

7.

8.

9.

10.

>TOURIST

NOTES

Made in the USA
Columbia, SC
17 December 2023